WRESTLING SUPERSTARS

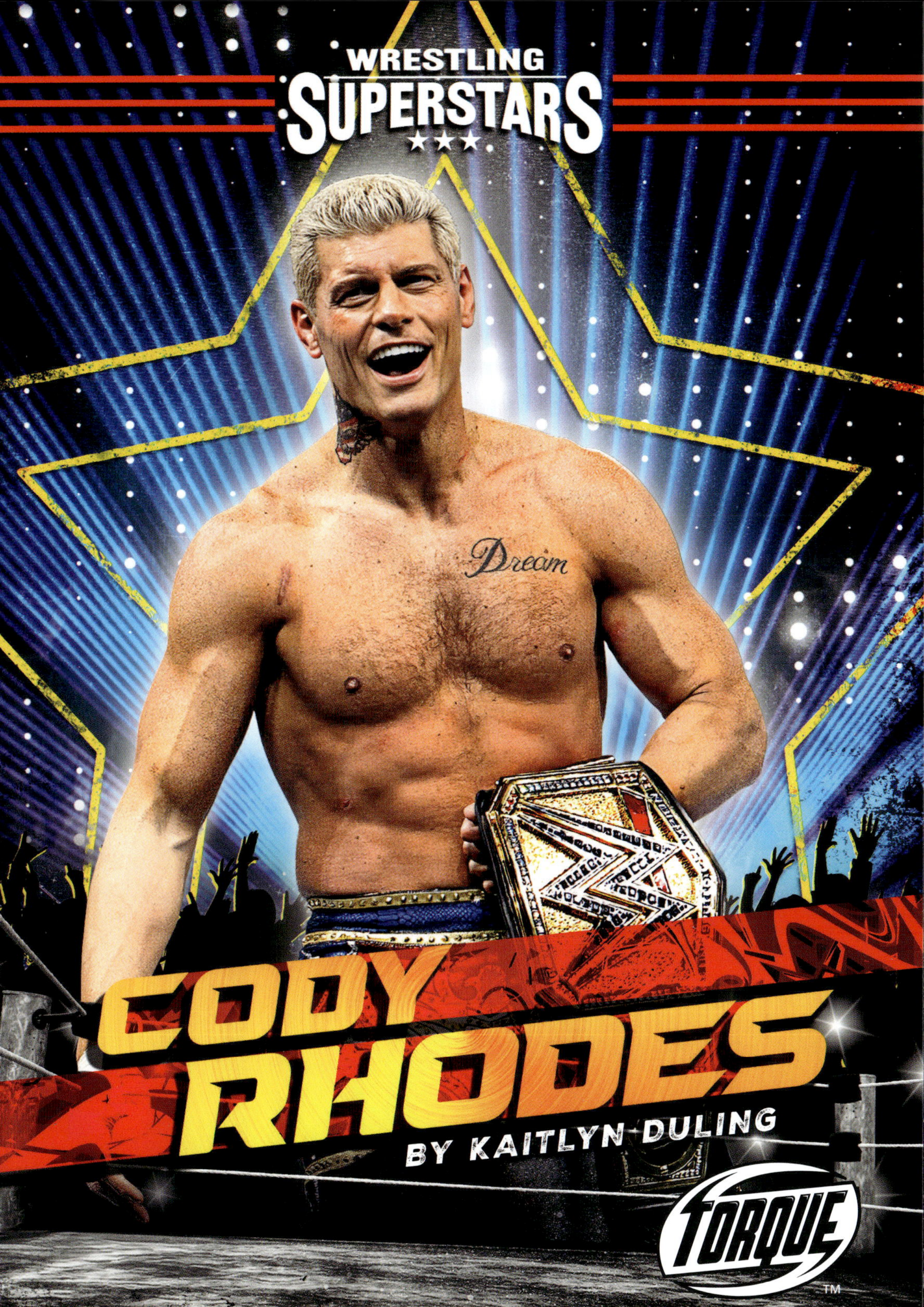

CODY RHODES

BY KAITLYN DULING

TORQUE™

TORQUE, AN IMPRINT OF BELLWETHER MEDIA BY FLUTTERBEE

Torque brims with excitement perfect for thrill-seekers of all kinds. Discover daring survival skills, explore uncharted worlds, and marvel at mighty engines and extreme sports. In *Torque* books, anything can happen. Are you ready?

This edition first published in 2027 by Bellwether Media, Inc.

For information regarding permission, write to Bellwether Media, Inc., Attention: Permissions Department, 3500 American Blvd W, Suite 150, Bloomington, MN 55431.

Library of Congress Cataloging-in-Publication Data is available at www.loc.gov or upon request from the publisher.

ISBN: 9798898801090 (hardcover)
ISBN: 9798898802332 (ebook)

Editor: Suzane Nguyen Series Designer: Gabriel Hilger

Printed in the United States of America, North Mankato, MN.

TABLE OF CONTENTS

RHODE TO GLORY

At WrestleMania 40, Cody Rhodes drags Roman Reigns to the middle of the ring. Cody uses his top move, Cross Rhodes. He slams Reigns down on the mat!

Cody throws Reigns to the mat one more time. The crowd counts to three. Cody has done it. He is the Undisputed WWE Universal Champion!

WHO IS CODY RHODES?

Cody Rhodes is a huge wrestling star. He has wrestled for over twenty years. He has been a **face** for **World Wrestling Entertainment (WWE)** and **All Elite Wrestling (AEW)**.

CODY RHODES

BIRTHDAY
JUNE 30, 1985

HOMETOWN
CHARLOTTE, NORTH CAROLINA

COMPANIES
WWE AND AEW

HEIGHT
6'2"

THEME SONG

"Kingdom"
Downstait

Cody is known for taking down **opponents** with his solo moves. He has been part of many **tag teams** too. He is a tag team champion!

GROWING UP IN THE RING

Cody was born into a famous wrestling family. His uncles, godfather, and dad, Dusty Rhodes, were well known. His brother Dustin is also a **professional** wrestler.

One of Cody's first memories was being in a wrestling ring. He traveled across the country to watch his family members wrestle. He watched them on videos and TV too.

CODY CELEBRATING WITH FRIENDS AND FAMILY

RAISED BY WRESTLERS

Cody spent time around many famous wrestlers as a child. Stone Cold Steve Austin once babysat him!

Cody showed star talent at a young age. Cody and his brother both wrestled in high school. Cody even won the Georgia state wrestling **tournament** twice!

Cody dreamed of being a professional wrestler. After high school, he went to acting school for one year. Then he decided it was time to follow his wrestling dreams.

CODY WITH HIS DAD, DUSTY AND BROTHER, DUSTIN

FAVORITES

DOG BREED

HUSKY

FOOD

WHITE RICE, GRILLED CHICKEN, AND THAI PEANUT SAUCE

CITY TO WRESTLE IN

PHILADELPHIA, PENNSYLVANIA

MOVIE

STAR WARS: EPISODE V – THE EMPIRE STRIKES BACK

WWE AND BEYOND

WWE RAW 2009

A BIG LOSS

Cody lost his first WWE match to Randy Orton, one of Dusty Rhodes's longtime opponents.

TIMELINE

2006
Cody signs with WWE

2016
Cody ends contract with WWE

Cody signed his first WWE **contract** in 2006. He joined a **developmental ring** in Kentucky. His first ring name was his birth name, Cody Runnels.

In 2007, he joined the show *WWE Raw*. He also started using his family's wrestling last name, Rhodes. He won some **matches** and lost others.

AEW

2019

Cody helps start AEW

2022

Cody returns to WWE at WrestleMania 38

2024

Cody wins his first WWE world title

THE LEGACY

STARDUST AND GOLDUST

In 2007, Cody won a WWE **title** in a tag team with Hardcore Holly. The next year, he turned **heel** and joined a **faction** called The Legacy.

In 2013, Cody and Dustin became a tag team. Their names were Stardust and Goldust. Eventually, Cody wanted more freedom to wrestle on his own. He left the tag team.

CODY AND BRANDI RHODES

BLING IN THE RING

Cody got married in 2013. His wife is former pro wrestler Brandi Rhodes.

WWE did not want Cody to leave the tag team. But Cody made a big decision in 2016. He ended his contract with WWE. He wrestled for **independent** companies. During this time, Cody took on the nickname The American Nightmare.

In 2019, Cody joined a company called AEW. He wrestled for AEW for several years.

LEAGUE LEADER

Cody helped start and run AEW as one of the company's leaders.

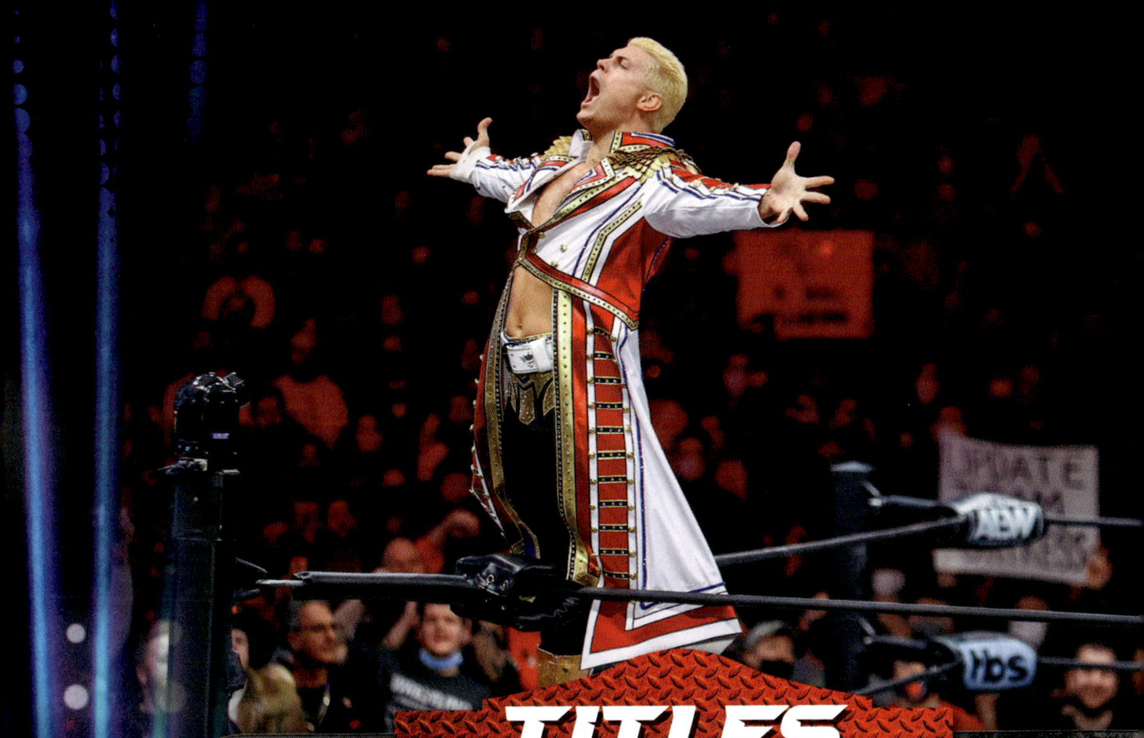

TITLES

as of 2025

2 UNDISPUTED WWE CHAMPION (FORMERLY CALLED WWE UNIVERSAL CHAMPION)

2X WWE CHAMPION

2X WWE ROYAL RUMBLE WINNER

7X WWE TAG TEAM CHAMPION

3X AEW TNT CHAMPION

Cody made his return to WWE at WrestleMania 38 in 2022. Cody defeated Seth Rollins! The following year at WrestleMania 39, Cody lost to Roman Reigns.

Cody wanted to win. At WrestleMania 40 in 2024, he challenged Reigns again. This time, Cody won! It was his first world title in WWE.

CODY AT WRESTLEMANIA 40

TOP MOVES

CROSS RHODES

GRABS THE OPPONENT'S TOP HALF AND FLIPS THEM ONTO THE MAT

CODY CUTTER

LAUNCHES OFF THE ROPES AND DRIVES THE OPPONENT'S FACE INTO THE MAT

BEAUTIFUL DISASTER

JUMPS OFF THE ROPES AND KICKS THE OPPONENT IN THE HEAD

TELLING HIS STORY

Cody wants to help other wrestlers. He owns a wrestling school in Georgia. People who want to become professional wrestlers can train at the school.

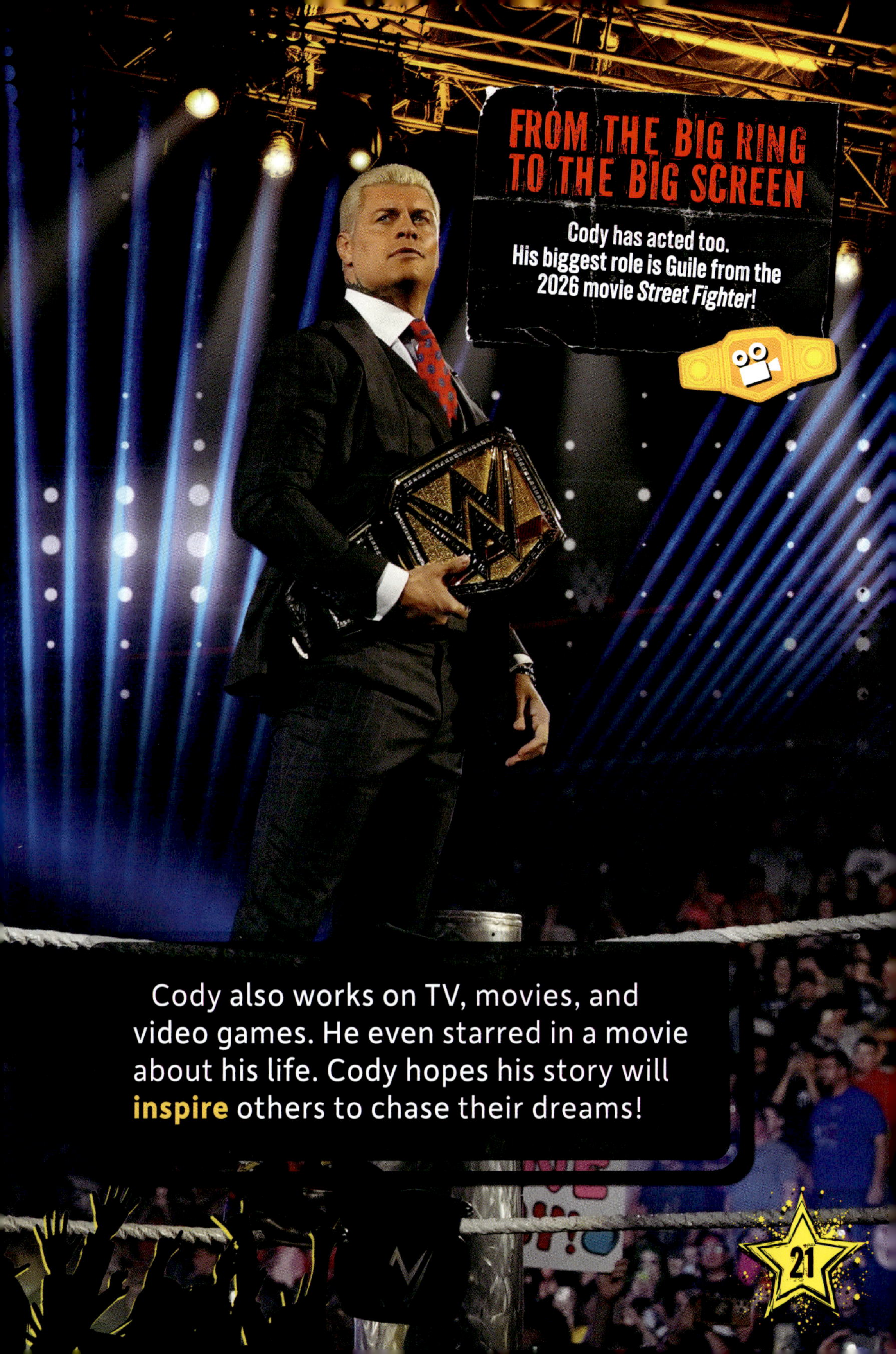

FROM THE BIG RING TO THE BIG SCREEN

Cody has acted too. His biggest role is Guile from the 2026 movie *Street Fighter*!

Cody also works on TV, movies, and video games. He even starred in a movie about his life. Cody hopes his story will **inspire** others to chase their dreams!

GLOSSARY

All Elite Wrestling (AEW)—a professional wrestling and sports entertainment company founded in 2019

contract—an official agreement

developmental ring—a place where new wrestlers can practice their skills before moving to a larger stage

face—a hero character

faction—a small group of wrestlers who band together

heel—a villain character

independent—not controlled by a larger organization

inspire—to make someone feel like they can do something

matches—contests between two wrestlers

opponents—people that wrestle against one another

professional—related to a person or athlete who makes money wrestling

tag teams—pairs or groups of wrestlers who wrestle as a team

title—the status of being the champion

tournament—a series of wrestling matches in which several wrestlers try to win the championship

World Wrestling Entertainment (WWE)—the world's largest professional wrestling and sports entertainment company

TO LEARN MORE

AT THE LIBRARY

Arnez, Lynda. *Be a Pro Wrestler*. Buffalo, N.Y.: Gareth Stevens Publishing, 2024.

Proudfit, Benjamin. *"The American Nightmare" Cody*. Buffalo, N.Y.: Gareth Stevens Publishing, 2022.

Smith, Elliott. *Steve Austin vs. Dwayne Johnson*. North Mankato, Minn.: Capstone Press, 2025.

ON THE WEB

FACTSURFER

Factsurfer.com gives you a safe, fun way to find more information.

1. Go to www.factsurfer.com
2. Enter "Cody Rhodes" into the search box and click 🔍.
3. Select your book cover to see a list of related content.

INDEX

The images in this book are reproduced through the courtesy of: diegofernandophotography/ Wikimedia Commons, front cover; WWE/ Contributor/ Getty Images, pp. 3, 4, 6, 7, 8, 9, 13 (2022), 18, 19 (all), 20, 21, 23; Tim Nwachukwu/ Staff/ Getty Images, p. 5 (top); Monica Herndon/ The Philadelphia Inquirer/ AP Images, p. 5 (bottom); ZUMA Press, Inc./ Alamy Stock Photo, p. 10; Edalin, p. 11 (husky); vaaseenaa, p. 11 (white rice, grilled chicken, and Thai peanut sauce); UpdateNerd/ Wikimedia Commons, p. 11 (Star Wars: Episode V - The Empire Strikes Back); Elsa/ Staff/ Getty Images, p. 11 (Cody Rhodes); WENN Rights Ltd/ Alamy Stock Photo, p. 12; Iruleitstrue/ Wikimedia Commons, p. 14 (top); Simon Hofmann/ Stringer/ Getty Images, p. 14 (bottom); Sipa USA/ Alamy Stock Photo, p. 15; Icon Sportswire/ Contributor/ Getty Images, pp. 16, 17.